and finally i've found peace

Denise F.

and finally i've found peace

and finally i've found peace

~2~

for m.

i loved you so much and despite
everything i am so grateful to be
able to get to know you
for a short time i was really happy
with you
i wish you that you also find your
peace and above all get rid of the
addiction
i hope you will be happy and one
day you will fight for love and not
just give up
i'll never forget you
i'm pretty sure of that
i really wish you the best
from the bottom of my heart. ♥

d.

and finally i've found peace

~3~

contents

you and me

and finally i've found peace

~5~

when i first saw you
i didn't think
that you would become
so important to me
i didn't think
that you would break my heart
but you did.

and finally i've found peace

~6~

i still remember
how we got to know each other
how charming and attentive you were
how you inquired about me
i would never have believed
that you conquer my heart
just to destroy it.

and finally i've found peace

~7~

that should never have been with us
and yet it happened
but i don't regret anything.

and finally i've found peace

~8~

do you remember
how we sat next to each other
at that moment
i forgot to breathe
at that moment
i knew
although it could not be
that i like you.

and finally i've found peace

~9~

i looked you in the eyes
and you in mine
your statement about it
that you realise that i like you
that my pupils are enlarged
my heart begins to race
then i knew
it's too late
i was completely in love with you.

and finally i've found peace

~10~

though we were strangers
we got closer every day
you knew exactly
what to write to make me smile
and unexpectedly
you became incredibly important to me
and my life changed suddenly
you became part of it.

and finally i've found peace

i remember everything you said to me
you've never felt like this before
you've never loved anyone sober
that i'm the right one for you
i know you were scared
but i was it too
because
i've never felt like this before either.

and finally i've found peace

~12~

i drove hours to spend time with you
how excited i was
my heart was racing
my breath stopped every time i saw you
and you felt the same way as me
you told me
and then you smiled at me
and all the tension was gone.

and finally i've found peace

you took my hand
as we walked under the stars
it was cold
and yet i was filled with warmth
i've never been so nervous before
and then
you turned me towards you
and placed your lips on mine
and my body got even warmer
fireworks ignited in my stomach
and all the self-doubt flew away
there was only you and me
and the clear night sky
with the shining moon
from then on i knew
i didn't want to lose you anymore.

and finally i've found peace

~14~

i remember the day like it was yesterday
we were in the car
we talked and laughed
we couldn't get enough of us
you told me how pretty i am
then you took my hand and wrote on it
if i wanted to be with you
it was a normal wednesday evening
and yet it was so different
i've never been happier
than when i was in the car with you.

and finally i've found peace

~15~

you told me
that you couldn't wait to see me again
i believed everything you said
i was so sure about us
and then
when you said that you love me
my heart started beating
that's when i knew i loved you too
really loved you
like i'd never loved anyone before.

and finally i've found peace

~16~

we weren't looking for each other
and still found.

and finally i've found peace

~17~

when i close my eyes
i see you standing in front of me
your brown eyes sparkle
your lips shine
your dark hair shimmers
i remember every detail of you
i hope i will never forget this sight.

and finally i've found peace

~18~

we are so different
that we are already the same.

and finally i've found peace

you gave me your sweater
the scent of your detergent hit my nose
and every time i was lonely
i picked up the sweater and thought
how thankful i am to have you.

and finally i've found peace

~20~

you called me every evening
we fell asleep together on the phone
that was the best part of the day.

and finally i've found peace

~21~

when we first slept together
i felt like it was my first time ever
and somehow it was.

and finally i've found peace

~22~

you sat on the chair and smiled at me
your smile is so beautiful.

and finally i've found peace

~23~

i remember your body
trained but not too much
i remember the necklace you wore
she suited you so well.

and finally i've found peace

~24~

i've never fallen in love with anyone
as quickly as i have with you.

and finally i've found peace

i remember exactly
when you hugged me for the first time
it was february
i accompanied you to the car
it was so cold outside
but when you took me in your arms
to say goodbye
the cold was suddenly gone.

and finally i've found peace

~26~

you stood in front of me
and tried to make an impression on me
and damn
it worked.

and finally i've found peace

~27~

no one can pronounce my name as
beautifully as you.

and finally i've found peace

~28~

you once asked me
if we wanted to go on vacation together
i couldn't imagine anything better
than traveling with you.

and finally i've found peace

~29~

hearing your voice
made my heart beat faster.

and finally i've found peace

~30~

everyone was so greedy
for your louis vuitton jacket
but not me
i was greedy for you.

and finally i've found peace

~31~

you once asked me
which type of chocolate i like the most
and i answered
i didn't think you would remember
but you bought me this chocolate.

and finally i've found peace

~32~

i remember
when you gave me your number
i couldn't wait to write with you.

and finally i've found peace

~33~

we weren't together long
hardly knew each other
but you became my safe place.

and finally i've found peace

~34~

you pulled me to you
kissed my forehead
and said
you love me
i felt so complete around you.

and finally i've found peace

you promised me
that i was more important to you
than drugs and alcohol
that you were incredibly grateful
to have me by your side
you told me about your past
how difficult that time was and still is
and i listened to you like always
you trusted me and i trusted you
and again
i believed you
it was april when i realized
it wasn't going to be as easy
as we thought
but at the time
i didn't think
that you would break my heart like that.

and finally i've found peace

broken

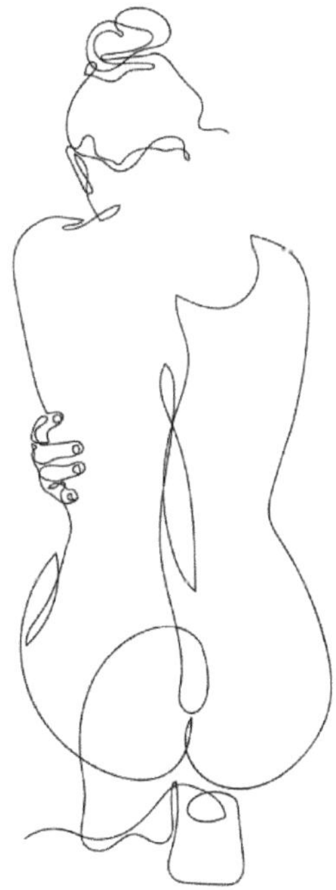

and finally i've found peace

you promised me so much
and kept nothing
i trusted you
and you lied to me
and yet
i loved you.

and finally i've found peace

i waited hours and days
to hear from you
and every time a part of me broke
all the excuses
all the lies
and i stayed with you
walked with you through your hard times
i put myself in the background
to be there for you
only to end up hearing
that i would never have supported you.

and finally i've found peace

~39~

do you remember
how we lay in bed together
me in your arms
it felt like home
how you whispered to me
that you love me
i wanted this night to never end
and now
i lie awake at night
with tears in my eyes
and i wish it was like that again.

and finally i've found peace

i had you by my side
then a part of you left
and in the end you were gone.

and finally i've found peace

~41~

i cooked for you
while you were on drugs
i was worried about how you were doing
while you were drinking alcohol
i thought how i could make you happy
while you'd rather be with your friends
i drove to you at night
just to wait hours in the car
for you to come
you told me you care about me
but i was only second choice.

and finally i've found peace

~42~

when we went for a walk at night
hand in hand
you said to me
that you wanted to leave
your old life behind
no drugs
no alcohol
but you don't have it
you'd rather leave me behind.

and finally i've found peace

~43~

the day you gave me roses and said
that's the first time
you gave someone flowers
i believed you because i loved you
how naive i was.

and finally i've found peace

~44~

you were up all night
to sleep during the day
i was waiting for you to wake up
that you contact me
to do something with you
but you didn't answer
only when the day was over
you have shifted me so many times
and in the end you blamed me
for never wanting to do anything
that i'm fucking boring.

and finally i've found peace

~45~

if i had known
that this would be the last time
i would see you
i would have held you in my arms
for so much longer.

and finally i've found peace

~46~

i fell in love with you
even though
you have so many problems
i fell in love with you
even though
you're addicted and dealing
i fell in love with you
even though
you're not at peace with yourself
i fell in love with you
even though
i knew it could break me
i fell in love with you
and you played with my feelings.

and finally i've found peace

you've been hurt so many times
and told me
you hate being hurt and lied to
by someone you love
then why did you hurt me so incredibly?

and finally i've found peace

~48~

i saw so much more in you
not who you pretend to be
it seems like
i was completely wrong about you.

and finally i've found peace

you texted me in the middle of the night
like usually
and i was awake listening to you
tried to be there for you
like always
thought how i can help you
how many thoughts i've had about you
but you didn't even think about me
i guess you didn't care.

and finally i've found peace

~50~

i hear your voice in my head all the time
she just won't stop talking.

and finally i've found peace

~51~

falling in love with you
was the best decision i've ever made
but also the worst.

and finally i've found peace

in my dreams we are still together.

and finally i've found peace

~53~

how many times have i sat in the car
closed my eyes
and thought about the moment
when you sat next to me
i miss these moments.

and finally i've found peace

~54~

and suddenly my home
didn't feel like home anymore.

and finally i've found peace

~55~

you once told me
that you wanted a future with me
that you want to have children with me
and never want to lose me
you asked me
if we wanted to move in together
was it all a lie?

and finally i've found peace

~56~

it's been eight months since i last saw you
i hope you were better off than me.

and finally i've found peace

~57~

you are like the stain
you left on my passenger seat
no matter how hard i brush
it just won't go away.

and finally i've found peace

~58~

maybe i gave you so much love
that you were afraid of it.

and finally i've found peace

~59~

before i knew you
i was happy with my life
why did you have to take that from me?

and finally i've found peace

~60~

i'm trapped
and i don't know if i can get out.

and finally i've found peace

~61~

you loved me
but somehow you didn't
you needed me
but somehow you didn't
you wanted a future with me
but somehow you didn't
it's like you want to be without me
but somehow with me too.

and finally i've found peace

~62~

what hurts so incredibly is
that i no longer know
what was real and what was fake.

and finally i've found peace

~63~

you already built our relationship on a lie
you said you would stay
but you left.

and finally i've found peace

and every shooting star i see
i wish you would contact me.

and finally i've found peace

~65~

you were online so many times
but ignored me for days
do you know how much that hurts?

and finally i've found peace

~66~

we wanted to go to the cinema
but you
just didn't pick up your phone anymore
i felt so betrayed.

and finally i've found peace

if only we'd talked to each other
the way i wanted
we could have saved so much.

and finally i've found peace

~68~

i miss touching you
i miss you so much
i hate it.

and finally i've found peace

~69~

02:00 a.m.   i'm awake
04:00 a.m.   i think of you
06:00 a.m.   i cry
12:00 p.m.   i should get up
03:00 p.m.   i'm still in bed
06:00 p.m.   i fall asleep
02:00 a.m.   i'm awake again.

and finally i've found peace

~70~

she is the girl who is decent
with a good family background and kind
he's the boy who is an addict
whose family split up early
and yet there was a spark between them
love knows no boundaries
love can only hurt so much.

and finally i've found peace

~71~

you were watching brooklyn nine-nine
on tv
when we spoke on the phone
you laughed and i laughed
for a moment we forgot
you were in therapy
for a brief moment
everything was normal.

and finally i've found peace

~72~

what happened to us?

and finally i've found peace

~73~

i've hoped so many times
that you'd text me drunk
tell me that you want me back
that you miss me
but you never did.

~73~

and finally i've found peace

~74~

sometimes
i listen to your voice messages
and fuck
i miss hearing your voice so much.

and finally i've found peace

~75~

words hurt
and i remember every single word
you said to me
and when i lie awake in bed at night
i think about it and wonder
if this will ever stop
i don't think so.

and finally i've found peace

~76~

when you told me
you gave a fuck about me
my heart broke at that moment.

and finally i've found peace

~77~

i tried to fight for us
i really tried
but i lost.

and finally i've found peace

~78~

i think i was never important to you
everything else
was more meaningful to you
drugs
alcohol
friends
money
then why did you want a future with me
only to drop me afterwards
and break my heart?

and finally i've found peace

~79~

you were the one who had feelings first
not me
but it's me now who's struggling with it.

and finally i've found peace

and suddenly
i became unimportant
all the effort
all the love i've had
everything flowed away like a river.

and finally i've found peace

~81~

you promised me
that you would never end this with us
now we go our separate ways.

and finally i've found peace

~82~

i loved your tattoos on your forearms
they were so meaningful
i just loved everything about you.

and finally i've found peace

~83~

why didn't you end it months earlier
if i was so fucked up?

and finally i've found peace

~84~

you claimed
that i had forbidden you so much
no alcohol
no drugs
when you used drugs in my bathroom
or at my dining table
when you bought beer every time we met
did i tell you not to take that shit
i can't remember doing that.

and finally i've found peace

~85~

i bought you that chocolate milk
you loved to drink
but this was never opened.

and finally i've found peace

~86~

dealing with drugs
was more important to you
than spending time with me
money was more important to you
than my love for you.

and finally i've found peace

~87~

as a kid i wanted to grow up
as soon as possible
now i wish i was a kid again.

and finally i've found peace

~88~

i opened my heart to you and you knew
how difficult it was for me to trust again
and you used it
you didn't care how painfully you broke it.

and finally i've found peace

~89~

you told me to fuck off
that i wasn't noble enough
that i have a shitty character
that i am an imposition
and stupid
have you ever thought about
how you were
and i stayed by your side
while i lost myself.

and finally i've found peace

~90~

maybe i fell in love with the idea of yours.

and finally i've found peace

you started making up lies about me
so you wouldn't have to admit
that it wasn't my fault
and i started to believe you
that i was to blame for everything.

and finally i've found peace

~92~

why didn't you fight for us
why did you just give up and left?

and finally i've found peace

~93~

suddenly i couldn't get up
i lay in bed all day
i probably wanted to escape from reality.

and finally i've found peace

~94~

although it's not true
sometimes i wish i'd never met you.

and finally i've found peace

~95~

i asked you
if you would like to continue
to be with me
you said you want
two hours later we were history
how is that possible?

and finally i've found peace

96~

when you left my life a part of me left too
i felt lost
i couldn't breathe anymore
have you ever loved me at all?

and finally i've found peace

~97~

i couldn't escape you
you were always on my mind.

and finally i've found peace

~98~

your sentences made absolutely no sense
i wonder how stoned you were
what drugs did you take
because otherwise
i can't explain
why you suddenly started
insulting me like that.

and finally i've found peace

~99~

i miss your 'good morning' messages.

and finally i've found peace

~100~

when did you decide to move on
without me?

and finally i've found peace

~101~

i never wanted to admit it to myself
but deep down i knew
it was going to end like this
i was hoping
things would be different with you
but unfortunately i was wrong.

and finally i've found peace

~102~

car rides in the middle of the night
the music playing at full volume
and tears in my eyes
this became a routine.

and finally i've found peace

~103~

tell me
do you think of me sometimes
tell me
do you miss me too?

and finally i've found peace

~104~

i wanted to do everything right
but i did so many things wrong.

and finally i've found peace

i have so much more
that i would like to tell you
but you never listened to me anyway.

and finally i've found peace

i feel sorry for the little girl
who was looking forward to growing up
the child who was always happy
where did she go?

and finally i've found peace

i would rather have stayed with you
despite my broken heart
than move away from you.

and finally i've found peace

~108~

you said you like writing with me
so why didn't you answer me then?

and finally i've found peace

i often wonder
why you had to ruin everything we had.

and finally i've found peace

~110~

i dreamed of you every night
and woke up with tears on my face.

and finally i've found peace

i would do anything
just to see you one last time.

and finally i've found peace

~112~

i've imagined so many times
what our future will be like
i think of the moments
we would have experienced together
how am i supposed to be able
to forget things
that never happened at all?

and finally i've found peace

"do you miss him?"
"no"
and then i started to cry.

and finally i've found peace

~114~

why do i always fall in love with people
who end up hurting me?

and finally i've found peace

your mom asked about me
even though she didn't know me
and in the end you tell me
that your parents never liked me?

and finally i've found peace

i wish i could kiss you again
and feel that tingling in my stomach.

and finally i've found peace

~117~

the saddest part is
that i don't even have a picture of us
you only exist in my imagination.

and finally i've found peace

~118~

i would have loved
to get to know you better
but you ended our chapter
like a book
that has been read to the end
and laid aside
you had already opened a new book
in which i don't appear.

and finally i've found peace

~119~

your best friend told you
i wasn't good enough for you
but he didn't even know me
then how can he know
that i'm not enough for you
and why do you even listen to him
and let yourself be manipulated like that
this isn't a real friend.

~119~

and finally i've found peace

~120~

i wrote you a letter to explain how i feel
it was hard for me to tell you
what's on my mind
you laughed at me
and flushed the letter down the toilet
was i worth nothing to you?

and finally i've found peace

a bad trait of mine is
that i think too much
what would have happened
if i hadn't given it so much thought
if i hadn't cared about your life
would you still be with me?

and finally i've found peace

i can't believe how wrong i was about you
i thought you were different
that you are worth it
but in the end
you are like everyone else
and this time
it hurts so much more
than the times before.

healing

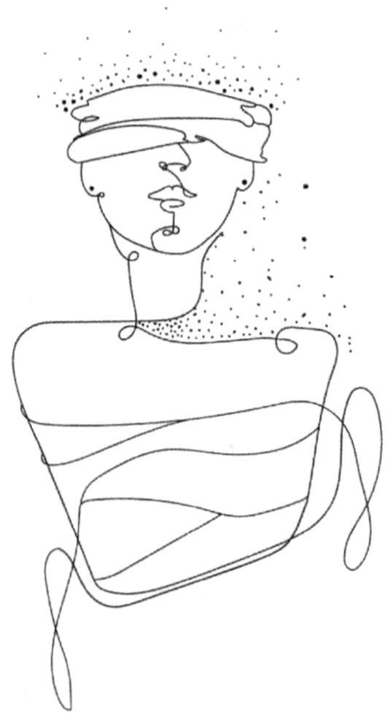

and finally i've found peace

it was june
the sky was cloudless
the sun burned my skin
the waves rushing in the sea
gulls flew around
children played in the sand
everyone was content
but not me
i wasn't happy
i just wanted to leave
i only felt the pain you left inside me.

and finally i've found peace

~125~

i often lie awake in the middle of the night
thinking of you with tears in my eyes
i often thought about
what i had done wrong
why you left me
even though you said
you love me more than anything.

and finally i've found peace

~126~

every day after you was a bad day
i missed you
every day
every hour
every second
i felt completely lost
and no matter what i tried
the tears just wouldn't stop.

and finally i've found peace

i thought about the time
when we kissed for the first time
under a clear starry sky
and like so often i wished
that i could turn back time.

and finally i've found peace

the thought of losing you forever
made my heart break again
anyway
i tried to keep going on
even if it should be without you.

and finally i've found peace

~129~

if you have to wonder if this is love
then you already know
it isn't.

and finally i've found peace

~130~

dear ex
you are lonelier than i thought
and i feel so sorry for you.

and finally i've found peace

step by step and you'll see
you'll be able to fly again.

and finally i've found peace

~132~

and soon the songs i hear
won't make me cry anymore.

and finally i've found peace

~133~

i find myself healing
because i no longer wish you the worst.

and finally i've found peace

~134~

your feelings were more important to me
than mine
and that was wrong.

and finally i've found peace

~135~

i don't think you've lost feelings for me
i think you know now
that you can never give me
what i deserve.

and finally i've found peace

one day everything will catch up with you
you will be devastated this time
you will be in despair
you will try to contact me
but i'll act like you then
be cold.

and finally i've found peace

~137~

you blamed me for everything
that actually shows
what kind of person you are.

and finally i've found peace

~138~

it may be the year of heartbreak
but it's also the year
of finding yourself again.

and finally i've found peace

drugs
alcohol
bipolar
adhd
impulse disorder
no job
dealer
probation
liar
and you think
you can easily find a new one
that stays like me
good luck with it.

and finally i've found peace

~140~

why did i stay
when i deserve so much better?

and finally i've found peace

~141~

you left
like it was the easiest thing
in the world for you
without thinking you hurt me
i wonder was it worth it
was that what you wanted?

and finally i've found peace

~142~

never to hear your voice again
smell your scent
hold your hand
feel your lips on mine
laugh together
hear that you love me
i didn't know it could hurt so much.

and finally i've found peace

~143~

i don't think
anyone will ever be able
to call me 'babe' again
without making me burst into tears.

and finally i've found peace

~144~

how can you go on
like nothing ever happened
like we never knew each other
while i'm breaking more every day.

and finally i've found peace

i never judged you
accepted you the way you are
tolerated your drugs
the alcohol
the excuses
why didn't you take me the way i am?

and finally i've found peace

you promised me
to spend more time with me again
that you would invest everything in us
was i really that blind with love?

and finally i've found peace

~147~

how many times i lay awake at night
stalking your social media
so many times the pain pierced me
as i watched you go on
while i dreaded each new day.

and finally i've found peace

~148~

i don't know why you blocked me
and then unblocked me
only to block me again afterwards
did you want to keep hurting me?

and finally i've found peace

i cried at night
it rained
and suddenly
rainy nights
became the ones
when i didn't feel anything
for you anymore
except anger and disappointment.

and finally i've found peace

~150~

the songs i heard reminded me of you
reminded me of us
i thought of you
but i couldn't stop hearing them.

and finally i've found peace

~

the days passed
and although i thought
i would never laugh again
i did
whether real or not
i could do it again
you hurt me so much
but you didn't break me.

and finally i've found peace

~152~

when you left a part of me died
i couldn't sleep
eat
laugh
i changed
i thought if i get like you
so cold and callous
i'll feel better
but that wasn't true
i just realized
that i never want to be like you.

and finally i've found peace

~153~

so many times
i thought i wasn't worth loving
that i'm unable to love
but afterwards i realized
that you are the one
who will never truly love.

and finally i've found peace

~154~

i thought i lost everything when you left
but i haven't
you are the one who lost everything
you're the one who ends up as a loser.

and finally i've found peace

i assumed i couldn't live without you
but i'd rather be without you
than with you.

and finally i've found peace

~156~

i believed in you when no one else did
but now it's time to believe in myself.

and finally i've found peace

because of you
i started to build a protective wall
around my heart
and no one will ever
break my heart again.

and finally i've found peace

~158~

i suffered so much after the breakup
at least that's what i thought
but actually
i suffered when we were still together.

and finally i've found peace

~159~

maybe i thought
it was nice to have you by my side
maybe
i didn't want to be alone
but i no longer stay with someone
just because it's comfortable
this is not a place that feels like home.

and finally i've found peace

actions speak louder than words
if you don't show me that you want me
then go.

and finally i've found peace

~161~

and even if you came back to me
it wouldn't be the same as it was.

and finally i've found peace

~162~

the thought of you
having another woman by your side
drove me crazy
but i realized
that she will only be your next victim
that you will treat her as badly as me.

and finally i've found peace

i am stronger than you think.

and finally i've found peace

~164~

the memories of you
fade a little more every day.

and finally i've found peace

~165~

you are afraid to take risks
you are afraid
that your facade will crumble
afraid to admit your feelings
maybe it didn't work out with us
because unlike you
i'm not afraid to take a risk.

and finally i've found peace

~166~

ever since you were gone
i've had you on my mind
tried to distract myself
celebrated
get drunk
meeting other boys
but it didn't help at all
it only got worse.

and finally i've found peace

we probably had different perspectives
when it comes to love.

and finally i've found peace

~168~

i'm not an experiment for you
to manipulate.

and finally i've found peace

~169~

i should stop making excuses for
why you are the way you are
i should stop defending you.

and finally i've found peace

~170~

you have no love inside you
except for yourself.

and finally i've found peace

~171~

i have accepted
that you will probably never
be mine again
and i'm totally fine with that.

and finally i've found peace

~172~

it was a beautiful love story that we had
it just wasn't written for us.

and finally i've found peace

~173~

all i wanted was to be there for you
but now it's time to put myself first.

and finally i've found peace

~174~

do you sometimes regret
how you treated me
i hope
your guilt will catch up with you one day.

and finally i've found peace

~175~

maybe
we weren't ready for each other yet
perhaps our story has yet to be written.

and finally i've found peace

i don't know
if that's your way of showing someone
you love them
it's definitely not my point of view.

and finally i've found peace

~177~

you're in such a bad position
you almost ended up in jail
even then i probably would have stayed
by your side
and would have supported you
where i can
you are absolutely right on one point
i'm really dumb.

and finally i've found peace

~178~

i've never been a fan of card games
but playing games
became a part of my therapy.

~178~

and finally i've found peace

~179~

it's sad
how much your addiction has changed you
at least it gave me a chance
to see who you really are
before it was too late.

and finally i've found peace

~180~

you didn't deserve my love.

and finally i've found peace

~181~

i have never mothered you
harassed you
or patronized you
i just wanted to be a part of your life.

~181~

and finally i've found peace

~182~

you wanted so badly
that we stay together
you said that your previous relationships
were broken by the addiction
but the dependency alone
was not the only problem
your character trait
is also partly to blame for everything
otherwise
it would have ended differently
with the two of us.

and finally i've found peace

~183~

now i'm sure
you were like that to me
because
you're afraid of what other people
think of you
your reputation is more important to you
than someone who loves you
accepts you as you are
you are afraid of commitment.

and finally i've found peace

~184~

i thought you were the love of my life
but i haven't found her yet
the love of my life is still waiting for me.

and finally i've found peace

i felt so free with you
like a butterfly
but now i realize
i was trapped
like a bird in a cage.

and finally i've found peace

~186~

you wrote me
that you already have a new girlfriend
although that wasn't true
can you actually do anything other
than just lie?

and finally i've found peace

the funny thing is
i don't hate you
even after everything you did to me
how could i hate you
when i once loved you so much
you are a part of my past
but now it's time to move on.

and finally i've found peace

maybe
it's not the end for us
maybe
someday we will get
to know each other again
maybe
we will fall in love a second time
and maybe
we learned something from the past
who knows what the future will bring
but now is not the right time for it.

peace

and finally i've found peace

~190~

my heart you broke into pieces
the scars you left
will probably never heal
they are a part of me now
but through you i learned
to love myself for who i am
that i don't have to change
i'm perfectly fine just the way i am.

and finally i've found peace

i always thought
you were the one who took my pain away
but in the end i realized
that it was you who caused me the pain.

and finally i've found peace

when i think of you now
i have a smile on my face
i smile
because i know i outlived you
that you'll never hurt me again
i smile because i'm glad
you won't be the man by my side
i now know
what i want
and what not
and i don't need you anymore.

and finally i've found peace

~193~

i have learned
that i am not a second choice
i don't have to let anyone
treat me that shitty
nobody deserves this.

and finally i've found peace

~194~

you have so many problems with yourself
i could never have helped you
and i don't have to break myself
to make you feel better.

and finally i've found peace

i would never have gone by myself
would never have had the strength
to leave you
so i thank you that it was you
who set me free.

and finally i've found peace

~196~

maybe i never missed you
just imagining
what could have been
if you had done
what you promised
but i doubt
it would have turned out differently.

and finally i've found peace

there's so much more in the world
to live for
than grieving over some guy
who's not even remotely worth living for.

and finally i've found peace

~198~

as i started to love myself again
i realized
that i was starting to forget you.

and finally i've found peace

~199~

we were strangers
then lovers
and then strangers again
but everything happens for a reason.

and finally i've found peace

what happened between us
was never my fault
i'm not perfect
but i haven't done anything wrong.

and finally i've found peace

~201~

you have such a negative attitude
towards life
that you almost dragged me
down with you
but i'm stronger than you
i was able to save myself.

and finally i've found peace

~202~

someday he'll show up again
maybe not right away
but he will
but don't forget how he treated you
how he broke you
while he give a shit about you.

and finally i've found peace

i don't need anyone in my life anymore
who doesn't appreciate or respect me
who only needs me when it suits
either all or nothing.

and finally i've found peace

~204~

thank you for giving up on us
the way is clear now for someone
who will really love me
and won't go
when things get tough.

and finally i've found peace

~205~

sometimes
love isn't enough
and losing me
just to make you feel good
that's not love.

and finally i've found peace

i thought you were perfect but
i always had the rose-colored glasses on
when i was with you
luckily
i finally took them off.

and finally i've found peace

~207~

you never apologized to me
and neither will you
but i don't expect it from you anymore
you are the way you are
a narcissist.

and finally i've found peace

~208~

and one day
i woke up with a smile on my face
i hadn't cried for days
i no longer feel the pain
that shot through my body
when i thought of you
then i realized
i finally let you go.

and finally i've found peace

maybe
someday you'll realize what you've lost
and maybe
you'll get in touch with me
i believe in second chances
but i'll never let myself break
like that again
it all made me grow.

and finally i've found peace

~210~

i still love you
but i love me more.

~210~

and finally i've found peace

~211~

even though i've let you go
something tells me
that we're not over yet.

and finally i've found peace

change is often difficult to accept
but it is worth it in the end.

and finally i've found peace

~213~

and at some point i stopped writing to you
to tell you that i miss you
it felt so liberating.

and finally i've found peace

it's okay to say 'no' sometimes
that doesn't mean you're a bad person.

and finally i've found peace

~215~

our chapter is finally closed
i am no longer dependent on you.

and finally i've found peace

you never know
what the next day has in store for you
but i am healthy
have a wonderful family
and great friends
life can be so beautiful
even without a man by my side.

and finally i've found peace

time doesn't always heal all wounds
that's true
but you learn to deal with them.

~217~

and finally i've found peace

~218~

you can't choose
who you fall in love with.

~218~

and finally i've found peace

~219~

never let anyone tell you
that you are not enough
because you're perfect
just the way you are.

and finally i've found peace

~220~

sometimes you have to go through hell
to realize how precious life is.

and finally i've found peace

~221~

and despite everything
i still believe in true love.

and finally i've found peace

~222~

nobody can tell you
how long you mourn someone
sometimes it only lasts days
sometimes months or years
be sad and angry
cry until no more tears come
but don't let sadness win out in the end
take your time and then
crawl out of your hole
and you'll be better sooner than you think
believe me
i made it too.

and finally i've found peace

~223~

i believe in karma
and that everyone deserves
what is due to them.

and finally i've found peace

~224~

showing your feelings isn't a weakness
it shows strength.

and finally i've found peace

~225~

from now on i only live in the present
not in the future
and certainly not in the past.

and finally i've found peace

~226~

i won't lie
even though you were so disgusting to me
you will always have a place in my heart
it just doesn't hurt me anymore.

and finally i've found peace

healing is like the ebb and flow
the tide comes in
and you think
you're choking with loneliness
but then the sadness disappears
the ebb has set in
and finally
you learn to swim at high tide
and stay afloat.

and finally i've found peace

~228~

in the end everything changes
for the better.

and finally i've found peace

~229~

no matter how hard it rains
no matter how hard it storms or snows
every day
you have the chance
to write a new chapter
in your own book
you are your own author in your life.

and finally i've found peace

~230~

even if i never thought of it
someday i'll be able
to love someone again.

and finally i've found peace

i wouldn't have believed that one day
i would be happy again
it takes time
i often had setbacks
and it hurts
so much
but i'm myself again.

and finally i've found peace

~232~

when you're feeling really bad you realize
who's there for you
who listen
is loyal
stays
and loves
luckily
i have people like that in my life
and i am so thankful for that.

~232~

and finally i've found peace

you were everything for me
i loved you incredibly
and somewhere i know
you me too
in your own way
i still think of you
and there are days
when i ask myself
'what if'
i will never forget you
but i can finally let go

~and finally i've found peace.

and finally i've found peace

and finally i've found peace

and finally i've found peace

a.

thank you for being by my side
thanks for listening
thank you for giving me advice
you are such a good friend
i hope i will never lose you
i am so lucky to know you
i love you
special agent a

d.

9 783000 742293